PRAISE FOR MARILYN KALLET'S POETRY

Packing Light: New and Selected Poems

"The ability to turn dross into gold is exactly the type of alchemy poets do. It is Kallet's Whitman-like embracing of pain and loss, be it the Holocaust, a mother's death, or simply those times where reality replaces dreams, that so fiercely connects readers with Kallet's poetry.

She has her following, to be sure, and part of her reader's commitment to her work stems from Kallet's commitment to blessing this world we have, not the one we wish it were, but the one in which we must live and learn to love."

—Charlotte Pence

Circe, After Hours

"Poetry is rarely audience-friendly. 'Serious' verse can be downright euthanizing, and puerile street rants against the corruption of everything only make us want to join the country club. So when a poet comes along who is funny, earthy, colorful and easy to understand, we sit up like Walt Whitman at the sight of bathing farmboys."

—*The Pitch*, Kansas City

"Marilyn Kallet writes with candor, infectious humor, and verve. Her poems keep delivering enjoyable jolts that you don't see coming... Kallet is a rewarding poet, willing to keep a reader regaled, an immensely skilled crafter of fat-free free verse."

—X.J. Kennedy

The Love That Moves Me

Poems by Marilyn Kallet

Marilyn Kallet

For Martin + Elena
Friedman, servi Burgess,
who know the
gusts of love that
move us —

Bises xoxo
love to the family
as well,
Marilyn
7/6/2013

BOOKS BY MARILYN KALLET

The Big Game, Benjamin Péret (translation)

Packing Light: New and Selected Poems (poetry)

Circe, After Hours (poetry)

Last Love Poems of Paul Eluard (translations)

The Movable Nest: A Mother/Daughter Companion
   (with K.S. Byer)

Jack the Healing Cat

The Art of College Teaching: 28 Takes (with A. Morgan)

One For Each Night: Chanukah Tales and Recipes

Sleeping With One Eye Open: Women Writers and the Art of
   Survival (with J. O. Cofer)

How to Get Heat Without Fire (poetry)

Worlds in Our Words: Contemporary American Women Writers
   (with P. Clark)

A House of Gathering: Poets on May Sarton's Poetry

Honest Simplicity in William Carlos Williams' "Asphodel, That
   Greeny Flower"

In the Great Night (poetry)

Devils Live So Near (poetry)

The Love That Moves Me

Poems by Marilyn Kallet

Joseph S. Phillips and Susan J. Wood, Ph.D., Publishers
www.blackwidowpress.com

Author photo: Christophe Gardner
Cover photo: *Beatrice in the Hall of Mirrors* by Melissa Morphew
Cover design: Kerrie Kemperman
Typesetting: Kerrie Kemperman

Woodcut, page 77, *Kapolohelele* by Dietrich Varez, is used by permission of the artist and the Volcano Art Center of Volcano, HI. All rights reserved.

ISBN-13: 978-0-9856122-8-3

Printed in the United States

10 9 8 7 6 5 4 3 2 1

For Lou and Heather, love again

ACKNOWLEDGMENTS

The following poems have been published in magazines and anthologies. Grateful acknowledgement is made to the editors:

Get This Right, Dog Days, *A Tapestry of Voices: Anthology of the Knoxville Writers' Guild*

I Want You Here, What Would Baudelaire Do?, Climbing Solo, *Blue Fifth Review*

River Talk, *Canary: An Online Journal of the Environmental Crisis*

When, Exclusive, Inferno Girl, Spleen, *Connotation: An Online Artifact*

Dear Emma, Eating the New Species, Confined, *Contrary Magazine*

My Sister on Hold, Few Talk, The Soothsayer, *Cutthroat: A Journal of the Arts*

Easy Listening Music first appeared in *How to Get Heat Without Fire*

Cons, *The Medulla Review*

You Are What You Haunt, Storm Warning, Love Poem for the Ageless, Uncle, That Chicken, *New Millennium Writings*

Blue Pie first appeared as Sweet Potato Pie in *Now & Then: The Appalachian Magazine;* reprinted in *Cornbread Nation 5: The Best of Southern Food Writing*

In the Shade of the Nuclear, *Outscapes: Writings on Fences and Frontiers*

Flamboyans, *Isotope: A Journal of Literary Nature and Science Writing*

Playing André, This Far, *New South*

At Red Cinder, Sirens, Detached, Lines I Can't Cross, *Peony Moon*

Soaked, *Plume*

Yom Kippur Remembrance, *PoetsUSA*

The Love That Moves Me, The Women's Version, Sad History at Dunes, Removed, Auvillar, Freeing Francesca, Sorcery, Complaint, *Prairie Schooner*

Orpheus Down Low, Euridice in Nelson County, *Rougarou, An Online Literary Journal*

Almost, *Still: The Journal*

Cons, The Love That Moves Me, Storm Warning, reprinted in *The Southern Poetry Anthology*, Volume IV: Tennessee

Dr. Robert Darwin Weighs In, *Valparaiso Poetry Review*

Old Teacher, *The Yalobusha Review*

Many of these poems were written with support from the Hodges Better English Fund and The Graduate School Professional Development Fund at the University of Tennessee. The Office of Research's Exhibit, Performance, and Publication Expenses Fund (EPPE) and the College of Arts & Sciences, with the Hodges Fund, have helped to support distribution of this book. Dr. Stan Garner, Head of English, and Dr. Carolyn Hodges, Dean of the Graduate School, have both been particularly supportive of my work, as have former department heads Dr. Chuck Maland and Dr. John Zomchick. My research assistant, poet Carolyn Stice, assisted with preparation of the manuscript.

The Virginia Center for the Creative Arts, in Sweet Briar and in France, has provided inspiration and hospitality for my poetry. Thanks especially to Sheila Pleasants, Director of Residencies, and to the Auvillar *directrice*, Cheryl Fortier. The villagers in Auvillar have nurtured me and my writing over the years. Special thanks to photographer and chef Christophe Gardner, to the Dassonvilles, the Brunes, Odette and Moïses Barratto (in memory), the McAllisters, to Francis and Jo at Le Petit Palais, and to poet Lucy Anderton and Jean-Phillipe Roux.

Much of "The Dreaming World" was composed on the Big Island of Hawai`i, at Red Cinder Creativity Center. Helen Chellin acted as a terrific guide and generous host. Garrett Hongo kindly helped me to sort out the Hawaiian diacritical marks. Dietrich Varez, beloved artist on the Big Island, graciously allowed me to reproduce his woodcut of Pele's sister Kapo in action; the image accompanies my poem "Detached." Emily Catey, curator at the Volcano Art Center promptly facilitated this permission. *Mahalo* to all of them!

Some of the third section, "Angel's Envy," was created at The Mary Anderson Center at Mount St. Francis in Indiana—a creative haven. Thanks especially to Friar Robert Baxter, the director of the order at the mount. Other poems in this section were written at The Porches, in Norwood, Virginia, thanks to Trudy Hale, and in New Harmony, Indiana, thanks to Laurel Smith.

Dr. Julia Demmin acted as a wise and thorough editor. Barbara Bogue, Pamela Uschuk, Deanna Kern Ludwin, Darren Jackson, Keith Norris and Tom Weiss made excellent suggestions. Poet Elaine Zimmerman contributed insightful notes. Heather Gross offered her impeccable copy editor's eye. Lou Gross gave loving, no-nonsense advice. I am tremendously grateful to these friends, writers, editors, and family members.

In a time when poetry and books are often undervalued, I am all the more fortunate to have Joe Phillips at Black Widow Press in my corner. His handsomely produced books set a standard. Gifted graphic designer Kerrie Kemperman enhances every volume. Thanks to these friends, and to those readers who still like to hold a book in their hands!

...amor mi mosse, che mi fa parlare.

The love that moved me makes me speak.

—Dante, *Inferno*

CONTENTS

II. The Dreaming World

III. Angel's Envy

PREFACE

Baudelaire is my boyfriend. He teased open poetry for me, gave me my first taste. Madame Pradal read aloud *"Correspondances"* in her theatrical voice—she had played the role of Phèdre in Paris—and I swooned. I was 18, a first-year student at Tufts, a poetry virgin for all intents and purposes. (Yeats and I had petted a little in high school.) Baudelaire in Georgette Pradal's mouth made me dizzy. I stared at the words on the page, tried to fathom how certain combinations of words and sounds could create such impact.

More than four decades later, I'm still fascinated by the ways that poetic sounds can transport the reader. Each spring I travel to France to write and to teach poetry for the Virginia Center for the Creative Arts in Auvillar. Not long ago, in my studio overlooking the Garonne, I composed "What Would Baudelaire Do?" The sensual atmosphere of the little village in Auvillar became palpable. Out of the shadows of the ancient walls stepped Charles B, and his most dangerous mistress, Jeanne Duval. *Vert et Blanc,* the "lure" in "What Would Baudelaire Do?" was my first real perfume, given to me for my nineteenth birthday by my first love. As I wrote, Baudelaire's adventures and my own intertwined, like the climbing rose vines on Rue Sainte Catherine. Over the next few weeks in Auvillar, the flowers grew swollen. One purple rose in Odette's garden at the top of the hill blossomed to the size of a child's head. Velvety siren! What would Baudelaire do? You know the answer! He would drink, write, make love to Jeanne Duval and to the white lady of "spiritual flesh," Apollonie. He would smoke hashish, travel "anywhere out of this world"—with wine, or poetry. With virtue? Not likely!

In the haunted 17th century bedroom where I slept during one of these residencies, I spent the hours before bed studying Dante in every translation I could find. For a long time I remained loyal to Ciardi's *Inferno*—that poetry rodeo—but the newer Hollander translation turns the Italian verses into idiomatic English and sings. That spring, I combed translation after translation, tested each line and syllable, and tried to read the Italian aloud in my New York accent. Then one evening as I lay in the haunted room, Beatrice started talking back to me. Thankfully, she spoke English.

Her presence in the poems persisted over several years. She murmured during boring faculty meetings. She and Dante bickered. It was stressful for them, finding themselves in East Tennessee. And I was an eavesdropper. Dante and Beatrice, Orpheus and Eurydice, and other famous couples with their mythic ups and downs have visited me in Knoxville, in Floyd's Knob, and in Virginia. Myths are portable and make for good company.

My residency at Red Cinder Creativity Center on the Big Island of Hawai`i did not include the presence of Beatrice or Eurydice. Pele, goddess of the volcanoes, rules that land. Her ups and downs, her blood pressure, may surge higher than the other women of myth, may grow hotter, increasing the risk level of all in her path, but she too knows heartbreak and loss involved in loving a human: the boiling lava of jealousy, the endless journeys to the underworld and back, to the snowy crest of Mauna Kea. Pele's adventures bring with them the risk of rising waves, of undersea journeys from which islands, creatures and people are born. Everyone who lives on the Big Island respects her and tries to stay out of her way, while giving thanks for the inspiration she insists on providing. I thanked her all the time, especially while drinking Lava Flows at the bar of Kilauea Lodge, tipped my hat to her awesome portrait hanging above the cozy fireplace. Her large earthen breasts made her seem like Madonna's Material Girl—they were no metaphor.

—Marilyn Kallet

I Want You Here

I Want You Here

So badly my fingertips ache
roses droop against the thorns

the green light of the Garonne
stuns my eyes

I talk to dogs   to my chair
listen at the neighbor's door

The old stones of the village are too smooth
The stubble of your chin will do

I want you here so badly
I can taste your salt

I'll save a place or two for your mouth
listen hard to your tongue

we'll coo like mad doves
become ballads   legends

climb to the *centre ville*
devour the first May cherries

pilgrims
at home in each other

beneath the blue sheet
of sky.

Exclusive

Je n'ai aimé que toi.
—Miossec

I loved no one but you, no,
and if the "only" before "you"
got stuck in my throat

like a Roy Orbison tune
or a wishbone,
whose fault was that?

I wrapped myself in our song
like a transparent raincoat.
What could I embrace

but the lyrics?
If I wore only song
and you came down in torrents

on another side of town,
of time,
if you were young, not too young—

I loved no one but you.
Well, almost no one.
Forgive me,

I was practicing.
Forgive the time
before you were born,

the Sixties, when
everyone loved everyone,
and by "loved" I mean *shtupped,*

and by everyone I mean Curly, Moe,
and Larry.
Once you came on the scene

I focused. I loved
no one but you,
no one—though you were

an *enfant terrible,*
terrible,
and I viewed you through

plate glass.
Now you're graying
at the temple.

Yes, the body is a temple.
Love,
let us pray.

What Would Baudelaire Do?

He'd gulp stars
& forgetting

prowl the *allée*
beg her thighs'

forgiveness
for a price

pray with his tongue
on her cat-tongue

spill cream
she'd lap

then smoke
inhaling long

outlive
his flesh   not his breath

her perfume
on the bureau

bottled lure, *chanson*
vert et blanc:

"Poet, I am not
all poison

drink my
éclat

behind the eyes
starburst of

souvenir
& yes

anywhere
out of this

world with
wine

poetry or
virtue, curled

in your
dark hair."

You Are What You Haunt

How I miss that shaky footbridge
between us, hours and miles when I

recomposed you. As if we could be.
If I am what I haunt then I'm a swarm of bees

in a dream of honey—you no longer exist without
my reaching arms. Restore the expanse between us

so I can spin the rope-bridge and
draw you stepping across it. In ancient days

I was the young one coming up the path,
angry at the *salé* who tried to muffle, to

mouth me in his image. But now
I sympathize with the grizzled wolf who snared me.

Now I haunt an image without hope, a terrible beauty,
indifferent, dazzling, cruel like a ravishing woman,

like a young man, like Rimbaud, and who am I,
Verlaine? And this is still life! This prison.

The Revolution

Why don't we do it in the road?

Honey, I don't grasp articles—
why's my chair feminine, wall masculine?
Stones.

Why is face masculine,
mouth mine?
Yours.

Land fog's masculine,
sea fog feminine?
We're lost.

Heart's male,
silence feminine?
You're the wall without a mouth in a fog.

Let's mess around.
I'll be your chair. Wall,
I'll scale you.

One caress by land, two by sea.
You're my mast in the fog.
We're the marshes,

trout, fishing hole, extra wine.
La la la! We're mixed-up nouns,
one imperative.

We're two raptors fucking in flight.
We're impossible, almost
out of breath.

Orpheus One and Two

Floating hair, wild eyes, Rimbaud's mirror.
He was the mold clay cried out for, proto-

Orpheus, unambiguous,
the cover shoot for Kubla Khan.

You barely escaped his flame in the day.
Melted down alone in your room

with a fistful of Halcion.
Time and milky weather finished off your

breasts, and later your four-year old
blurted, "Mama, do you love someone

besides Daddy?"
Now the bard has buzz-cut

his right-minded head
to silver fuzz. He utters measured tones,

making amends. Nothing's left
of the Big O who drove your poems.

For years, he'd show up in dreams as
Crazy Dog, and you kept opening your hand

To his incisors. Scene Two, twenty years
down the pike, you invite him back in.

Harmless now, right? He acted Orpheus
until the new kid grabbed the part. What may undo

you is not this elder statesman by your side,
but your desire to prove to the ingénue,

young Orfée, that you don't need
his fucking hair, his bowed lips.

You can ignite words
sin otro, sin—if it takes the whole

Foreign Legion, or one man.
Arm-in-arm with the arch flame-thrower,

the Cadillac Coupe of muses, you'll show him,
make him tear with his teeth the pulp

his poems are written on, cut his new poetry
paper doll out of the rosy picture—

Reader, are you confused? I suppose you've
never tried to make a new flame jealous

with the oldie? At least you'd be sure the ashes
were out, stomp, stomp, over,

calling Orpheus One, Orpheus Two,
over, (Paris is burning in its skin)

(almost)
out.

High Cost Blues

You know you're lost when you buy his ex-wife's *parfum*
graze yourself lightly under your dress.
You're resorting to trickery and ruse, slipping his name
into random sentences with office staff.

You graze your inner thigh with scent,
drop his name as if it held no weight,
slip it into random sentences with staff,
hope they don't notice you're reddening.

Drop his name as if it held no weight,
no ammo. Bashō would not
have okayed this flash and boom.
Silk, velvet, perfume—why so rough?

You know you're resorting to trickery, to ruse,
you're lost, swathed in *J'adore*! His ex-flame's.

Cracked

He's a nasty-looking customer.
She has the jowl of fish.

He looks a bit of a mug.
She's a blockhead.

To go crackers.
Goatsucker.

Bless her heart, how can she suck goat
with her jowl of fish?

Through prayer.
Two-headed monster.

"She has a good head on her shoulders."
Code!

Mr. McCall down the block,
career British army,

wants to tell me something.
But what?

Bullethead (*Tête ronde*).
Hangdog look (*Tête basse*).

to dine alone together
(*Tête-a-tête*).

That's it! Mr. McCall
(Nigel) wants us to dine

alone together,
without the formidable wife.

She rereads Pétain's speeches,
used to be known as "Madame Peepee,"

she had the key to the loo.
Has Nigel taken leave of his senses?

Il a la tête montée.
His blood is up.

Me? I have a headache.
Head to foot.

Playing André

I am playing André Breton
to your Joyce Mansour,

by the book this time.
No sampling the goods,

though mourning doves in the garden
coo throatily.

Unlike André I am not *scandalisé*
by mechanical toys—*au contraire!*

You're working me and I know it,
gaming and scheming,

never enough.
André and J might have felt this way,

yearning their loyal companion
as they toured the Loire Valley,

haunting the marvelous.
Not in the skin,

no, love was all lines,
literary passion.

Just as well, Puritans
tossing vibrators into the incinerator.

Where's Eluard when we girls
need him?

Artaud's burning at the stake, Desnos
nods at the wheel, and no matter how

I fudge the verbs *en français,* mix
hours, years, *heures, années,* we'll never

arrive together, baby,
not even manually.

That Chicken

Was a senior citizen,
an octogenarian,
the oldest one in Valence d'Agen.
That chicken's skin was so thick
it couldn't be insulted,
not even by a knife.
That chicken was so old
it knew my Grandma Anna in Minsk.

That chicken was so tough
even the boiling water complained.
That chicken wasn't worth fifteen euros.
Fifteen! That chicken was tougher than the pot,
tougher than the teenage boys
who rumbled last night by the dock,
and much less sexy.

That chicken was one of two on Noah's ark.
I ate it because I paid for it.
Each bite was an insult.
That was the chicken they saved for the American.
That was the chicken that broke détente.

I made a soup of it,
and with enough hours and white wine
even the oldest clucking citizen of the republic
gave way to my teeth.
With a loaf of olive bread to distract me
I polished off that beast.
But was it a chicken or a buzzard?
Je m'en fous! For fifteen euros I'd eat a hedgehog
if it landed in my shopping bag.
I'm no spring chicken,
but I'm livelier than that old bird.

Love Poem for the Ageless

If we were ageless and wore no bodies, we could rendezvous on a slip
of light, a firefly's back—no one would begrudge us,
and my face wouldn't crack—

No more death mask jokes, no
punch line
blows.

Who crumbles from them? Not Ozymandius,
not any object, present or past.
Me, my pretensions, who did I think I was?

I'll be out of time
soon enough.
Stick to that, that time of year,

bare.
If we were ageless, bodiless,
outside ourselves,

we'd meet like this, in words,
pinpricks of light—
this other real

almost-flesh.

My Poison

American bug spray shoots more poison than the French,
more John Wayne than Sarcozy,

but this is a screen for what
I wanted to write about you, Pet,

about not wiping me out too soon.
If I think about you less, Dear Poison,

will that stop you from annihilating me?
Verlaine is writing to Rimbaud from a café

so his wife won't clobber him with a fry pan.
V needs the bourgeois bed and Madame's

steady income. Rimbaud adores Verlaine's
bankroll, and is not about to say goodbye.

So on this July day, it's likely Verlaine
who cries *you're killing me, I can't take it.*

Likely Rimbaud tries to stop him,
and not the way the history books

frame the aging queen.
Dear Mosquito, dear Infernal Pest,

only one of them
pulls a gun.

Annoying and Winged on the Garonne

They sound off like tugboats, *mais non!*
Blaring, they're turtledoves,
tourterelles, honking like mad taxis.
They'd be taken down in Manhattan.

Blaring like whacked-out cabs,
they'd be blasted downtown, sautéed
in Chelsea. They couldn't hack
Avenue B, street-grade wings,

con chiles. Buttered in Chelsea.
Fried quicker than jacked-up taxis,
these birds wouldn't last a beat on B.
They'd give poets and drunks a migraine.

Downed, beer-battered, not tugs.
Antipasto.

When

When the low heavy sky weighs down like a cover, you're in Auvillar
without your spouse. Dante's on his way.

Ladies of a certain age compete for clothesline.
Show off gleaming copper pots.

Tea and flan, wet wash. Dante's
not your concern.

Beatrice tends him,
pats dry.

Push past your fears, Francesca!
Seize the line while Madame snores.

Twist your fingers through Dante's damp curls.
He'll know what hit him.

Then run run run under grey skies.
You have feet, orthotics.

Sadness that rivals rain.
Blue clothespins

can't clasp your tidy life
if you're in the wind

with him.

Voyant/Voyeur

Buttons are windows, you claim, & I lean
to peer through yours, crave
a better view, fresh air, fresh something.
You self-correct, "Nipples
are windows. Air is dream."
Hmmm.

That's your excuse? You needed air
so you opened
her windows with your tongue? I'm
wrestling with your metaphor,
Monsieur! I agree that poets
breathe dreams, but the rest?

You accuse my vocabulary
of being scantier than my negligee!
Shy buttons, not nipples, you insist,
unlock her. Pajamas, panoramas.
I understand, Monsieur,
French women promise lotus-eating,

rare perfumes,
drunken voyages, dreams
of deeper journeys
Orpheus strummed
into the turbulent eye of Eurydice
and down,

into the dark well
of rending and oblivion.
Head and limbs at odds,

torn by cast-off women.
Furies? I've been
furious with you a time or two myself,

Monsieur. Now I want to toss back
dreams, tear off the buttons,
lids of closed portholes,
throw aside caution,
grasp you
like a mariner

who has veered too long
from port. I am no Saint Catherine,
Monsieur, but would welcome
your roving lips on my pink buttons,
help you hoist that heavy
tricolor.

Storm Warning

I am the queen of a rainy country
whose king has gone dark.
He's a speechless river
but I have not stopped listening.

The king left his voice somewhere else,
holds his cruelty close.
I have not stopped listening—
thunder, roar of the rising river.

More wall. His cruelty
huge and other-worldly.
The swollen river breaches the banks.
Indifferent gaze behind the weather.

He is the sullen king of elsewhere.
I am queen of a country where the wall is gathering.

Pitiless

I want you   here

    here   and o yes

down

    here

    river is swallowed

   by motors   *rhrhrh*

    &

cannot sing

   to love that   *to love*

well which   *which*

   which

thou   must

   leave   *(ere long)*

      thou

I should never have   ached for

  on the day   they

drowned

I want you

here   but who gets

what   they

(the river)   did

gulped a family

       entiére

(greedy) impassive   river

Why
      Why guzzle

whole?   Why not strike

father   or

firstborn   terrible

    mouth of the river—

weeds below?

the little ones   sippycups

swallowed   swallowing

Why cram down mother, too

and the wombful

Why not leave someone

to   *greee*

Oral History: The Soothsayer

I have come here for this,
to walk down the rocky slope
by the river,
near the seer's place.
"*Bonjour!*" I call out.
"Are you a believer?" she asks.
"Yes!"

Her rooms reek of cat piss.
Marie-Louise reveals her collection
of shells and a trilobite,
five hundred million years old.
"Are you the one who knows things?"
"*Oui!*" she replies.
She'll use cards and a pendulum.

"Do the shells talk to you?"
She looks at me like I'm crazy.
"I'm the one who talks," she responds,
"with God's help."

Ninety-two, nearly blind,
she offers a lemon ice cream cone,
and purrs, licking hers.
Talks about saving Jews in Moissac.
Says the gendarmes brought Jews
to her house, ordered her family to hide them.
Risky, gathering food for so many.
Sometimes they hid the Jews in the pig sty,
or in a hole under a woodshed.
At night the Jews stepped outside to breathe.

One day, at the market, a neighbor pointed to her
and yelled, "They're hiding Jews!"
She bursts into tears.
That night the Jews had to flee.
"Were they saved?" I ask.
"*Oui.*" But she is crying too hard to speak.

She rummages for photos of Laroquette,
the house where the Jews hid,
another of her handsome husband José.
He was Portuguese, the marriage
arranged.
Marie-Louise had been "*abusée*"
by an uncle.
Her mother didn't believe her.
"*C'était affreux!*" she says. "*Affreux!*"
She was ruined, the marriage
hurried. "Forty-two years with José,
I never loved him."

She holds up the pendulum,
with its faces of Buddha, Jesus, and Ra.
When I tear out of her house I gasp
fresh air by the river,
toss back a few glasses of Sancerre.

For twenty euros, for you, too,
the pendulum will swing, "Yes,"
"No," "I will not answer."
The seer's window opens on the
good police, the bad uncle,
lost Jews and the current of tears.
Visit soon. What the seer knows
will soon be gone in the grey-green waters
of the Garonne.

Sad History at Dunes

When I trouble him again about the Jews at Dunes,
Moïses winces. "*Oui,* twelve were hanged
in front of the mayor's office,

three days after the war had ended."
Villagers pretended not to hear
about German surrender.

"Even today those rednecks stay ignorant,
illiterate, gung ho.
Collaborators!"

Moïses himself was denounced in Dunes,
beaten, jailed. Tried to escape.
Part of his foot was blown off.

"I received no medical treatment
for over a year. My buddies carried me out
to watch the Liberation!"

After the war he studied couture
in Paris, won highest honors
as a tailor. Worked as a tailor at a chateau

until guild members grew jealous.
In his home-sewn silk suit,
impeccable, this 86 year-old is dapper.

He adores Edith Piaf and Josephine Baker.
He used to sing tenor.
Loves to joke, to make people think

he's lost his senses in silliness.
"I've known so much suffering—
I need laughter."

His hidden garden is filled with sculptures
of nests and long-legged birds.
His wife Odette tends green rows

overflowing with roses
and sweet basil,
calming vervain. "I've had no relief

from pain since the war," he confides.
He won't return to Dunes.
Those who denounced him

were never punished.
"Justice is rotten. Rotten!"
he groans.

River Talk

When I let the river answer it babbles
    barges, hooks, oars,
undertows.
    It surges kings and arms,
Black Death, Jews, witches,
    poison, smell of burning,
confides: heroes,
    collaborators, pyres.
When I let the river answer it
    obsesses about the
nuclear plant upstream.
    Rivers speak to other rivers.
 When the earth trembles
    even rivulets feel shaky
in their crevasses.

When the fish sicken,
    the river can't arise and leave.
Saules along the bank weep.
    Doves *hoo-hoo* like captains
minding the harbor.
    The river's never fooled.
The Garonne stays stubborn,
    surges despite pizza vans and dumps,
despite bridges and Peugeots racing overhead.
    It gazes at the white sky
and reflects, mouths
    slick rocks, lightning and shifting
banks, fish skeletons,
    drowned boys, drought, dust,
softened earth,
    grass waving *bye!* like Samson's locks.

This Far

You're lucky, lucky to have come this far.
You survived molten skies

and ash.   You've come for Dante.
He's up front about bringing her.

Beatrice. Duh.
You wish she had not tweeted her daughter's

shoe size. That he
was not a Puritan.

In the distance,
foghorns.

Ships have long abandoned the canal.
Can it be the nuclear plant?

So soon?
Somewhere, someone gets lucky.

Under the circumstances,
it will not be you.

I Am the Wound and the Knife

> *Je suis la plaie et le couteau…*
> —Baudelaire

Today the wound,
   the air around me
emptied

twenty years ago

Dante spotted Beatrice
   who eventually greeted him

not you
   though

Even the knife needs flesh,
son

you are saving yourself

> *Tous les êtres aimés*
> *Sont des vases de fiel qu'on boit les yeux fermés.*

all loved ones are vases
   this one rife with vervain

and we are in a swoon
   eyes shut

this one   empty   something flown
   not speaking   gall or gull

this one

Bitter is the wisdom   gained
   voyaging

and that dish ran away with
   the spoon   and the knife

ran away with the blonde
   and the wound

sang until it forgot
   le sang

lucky little cut
   sang until it forgot.

In the Shade of the Nuclear

Auvillar, 2007

stries,

        streaks   layers

   the Garonne

     mirror of the *saules*

         willows

   water pulsing

out of view   the nuclear plant

   with its tall bursts of

we hope (steam)

only Americans speak of

Three Mile Island

Chernobyl

        The French are more *accompli*

        the Jersey mob doesn't own the

        construction

nevertheless   in Japan (Kashiwazaki)

        an earthquake

        startled a plant

built on a fault line

        an engineer will be

shaken if not ka-bobbed

and we Americans are taking photos

of spiderwebs on the bridge in moonlight

huge arachnids   we don't want

        to run our hands along the railing

teens joyriding at 100 km

        won't kill us

we trust our American   arachnidean luck

too naïve

to be headlines

* * *

"the nuclear plant is only visible from
one view"   our orientation packet promises
and from the others, roses   yellow, red
perfumed coral
                    Mama!
It was she, in the shadow of the
poverty and violence that buffeted us
                    who made roses spring
she held the source in her green fingers   shaped her oasis
I'm told the old house has been demolished
but I visit   in the wide-open roses

Down the block the nuclear blooms, too
two plants eject white steam   invite picnics on a sunny day
and the locals have more jobs   and cars
and TV's you can see the flicker of tubes through
openings in 12th century walls

and we all want to watch   we are tempted to break into
people's homes to catch the news
pixel-hungry Americans
                                   "Japanese concerned over
nuclear safety,"   a bit late, what?
the largest nuclear plant in the world
                    built on a fault line
then the earthquake   "How could they have not
known?"   the earthquake defied expectations
"struck with a broad, wrenching, horizontal swaying
that caused water to slosh out of pools."
Hitoshi Sato, deputy director general of safety
said, "If you insisted on being 100 per cent sure
about finding all active fault lines, you'd never get
anything built."

So there you are, *Mesdames, Messieurs,*
it's a crap shoot   down the block

drink your Bordeaux, 2005,
only four euros in the Casino   don't sweat
the nuclear   you can't control
locals pour vodka and coffee for breakfast
champagne overflows the supermarket shelves

as long as the Garonne is not sloshing
the earth is not trembling
go have a little *apéro*
and it will be nice   a little walk
where the Saint Jacques   went before you
and then lost his head   as you will
when Stéfane leans his curly head over the ruins,
"Hallo!"

Leaving the House, Auvillar

"The door itself / makes no promises. / It is only a door."

You go out in search of news and some air. Ashes have been censored by American newspapers. Best not to mention ashes too soon. At certain altitudes, day is black like night, says *Le Monde*. Volcano sky.

Crows thrive, size of hawks. And the constant bird song? "*Merles,*" someone explains. Madame Merle inhabits an ancient apartment with her cats. Madame Blackbird. Wait, don't arrive at blackbirds yet. Creep up on them like Vegas. Maybe that old feline will get lucky. She senses you and scats, knows where the hidden patch of sunlight warms cobblestones.

You seek Baudelaire at the end of your alley but only tourists and pilgrims appear. Some of the pilgrims have rented fat donkeys. Cheaper to run than a Citroën. Another cat dashes by with a small black creature dangling from its jaws.

A few Righteous families in Auvillar hid Jews. Those Hidden Children are in their seventies and eighties now. One couple lives in Florida, and though they have email, you have not made contact. Waiting them out? *Je suis desolée!* Now we have arrived at ashes and those still breathing. What to say? Hello, I am in the village that hid you but not others?

C'est la vie, the old women repeat. Or not. If you were a wealthy doctor in 1942, and boasted, named your house Le Chateau, maybe one of those women told the Germans where to find your wife. After so many years, why stay angry at the *mairie?*

These days, Auschwitz is a tourist trap, someone remarks. Be grateful the villagers saved your children! Your son became a doctor, too, with his fancy Paris office. White-haired, your daughter resides near Versailles, afraid of leaving the house, terrified of her door. Village elders shake their heads at the mention of her name. *Dommage!* What a pity, they sigh.

Get This Right

Non, the alderman said, *numéro trois, Place de l'Horloge.*
The Jews used to live near the butcher's,
not the soap shop.   I thanked him.
Need to get this right.

Adéle Kurzweil tried to study there, before the butchery,
before gendarmes seized her.
Get this right. Fleeing Austria, Bruno, Gisele and their daughter
tried to live in Auvillar—their papers in order. After Wansee,

the Final Solution, gendarmes grabbed them,
chained off *numéro trois, Place de l'Horloge.*
Fleeing one, two round-ups. Their papers were in order.
Adele dropped her history book. Drancy. Septfois. Auschwitz.

Not the *savonnerie.* I thanked him.
No mistake. "Kurtzweil. Number 3. Place of the Clock."

Few Talk

Mémoire et Espoirs de la Résistance

Few here talk
about the 400 young Jews saved.

1943, nine-year-old Jean Raphael Hirsch,
alias "Nano," pedaled his bike

from Auvillar to Moissac,
his satchel packed with *biftek*.

Beefsteak, they called the false
papers and passports. Nano

was not home, October 18, 1943,
when the Nazis seized his parents.

Auschwitz. His mother, 37, was gassed.
After the war, his father testified against Mengele.

Jean Raphael was hidden in the convent
of Auvillar, and then by Dr. Daniel,

who cared for the wounded.
That's why Nano became a doctor, he testified.

Today in Auvillar, no one speaks of these heroes.
"Oh, everyone claims to have been in the Resistance!"

one villager scoffs. "Those who collaborated
might get their feelings hurt," another explains.

Jean Raphael remembered that local farmers
hid the fleeing German Jews.

All four hundred escaped,
he swore.

So every villager breathed complicit air,
for a moment,

breathed the air
of the Just.

My Sister On Hold

This morning our parents were milling about,
more cheerful

than alive.
In and out of the kitchen,

they murmured.
Lights burned,

windows stayed open.
No one complained.

As I drifted out of sleep,
I told myself, "Remember

that you have seen them."
We moved together

in a painless stream,
a family again,

without *tsuras.*
We were fluid,

the way others might remember us
if they were generous—

buoyant and secure
in the current.

Odd, though, I didn't see my sister.
She lives too far away,

in Connecticut,
busy

at the legislature.
Me, I floated in heaven,

firstborn!

What I've Learned from Hanging Wash

Auvillar

She who wakes early gets a spot in the sun.
She who tarries sleeps on damp sheets.

Clothespins play chameleons in tall grass.
Don't keep checking to see what's dry.

Shake out the sheets or snooze with spiders.
Other people's underwear is sexier than one's own.

If a mouse enters with your pillowcase,
toss *le petit* out the window.

Others will avenge him in your armoire,
nibble peepholes in your linen pants.

Your mother pinned up four times
as much wet wash, every day. She wasn't on

a chic Provençal vacation.
Too late to tell her you understand.

Just get it done.
If others hog the sun, don't fuss.

Bad karma to argue over laundry.
Good form to quarrel over film noir.

Pour a glass of Sancerre.
at dusk. *L'Chayim!*

The first night on clean sheets
enfolds you, lullaby of sun.

The Women's Version

I was doing the women's version
of *Death in Venice*—

                (Valence d'Agen)

had stayed too long
in the flu zone
long after the *Garde nationale*
arrived—

not on the chance
of seeing the swine,
but because I knew he
liked thinking of me
there—

nel mezzo   past
                              midway

nothing says fun like midway
but   only
                              in France

the women guard
their men

with red nails

                              the Dobermans
                              with bat ears

can be sweet
guarding their motorcycle men

"philanderers"   I think she said
philosophes?
they cheat   *pas de problème*

Without my cell
I was no better than Jean-Paul Sartre
cut off, alone—

I fell victim to Stockholm
syndrome with
the entire Delta flight crew

and with everyone else
here
in town—

the supermarket clerk
new best friend
until I simpered,

Ne troublez-vous pas!
"Don't double yourself!"
Non! she growled.

I wanted to marry one
of them, but
which one?

Stéfane says
he didn't remember me,
but he does now.

Beatrice's *Inferno.*

The Love that Moves Me

amor mi mosse...

Makes me speak. Or is this
some lesser muse, that he-beast
with reeking innards?

Goth, I know!
Why call for answers
if love's divine?

Why not worship like *el maestro,*
a glimpse of his beloved?
Beatrice cupped vision in words.

Virgil spoke up.
Had he held still
there would have been no book,

no hell, heaven, souls.
Now every church in Florence
has their number, every schoolgirl.

I'm well past the middle of my life,
less able to cast visions
on a still life.

I won't scold.
Let's admire the blank
you have created,

the sea of silence that surrounds you,
the taciturn mountain
you climb daily.

I won't ask for hello.
That would show lack of faith.
Let the song be my mojo,

the *terza* save me from wraiths,
rima not take me down.
Be my Virgil if not my angel.

If not my divine *amor,*
I might settle
for gutsy love.

Freeing Francesca

It wasn't God who made honky-tonk angels.

"For pity's sake,
    Francesca, time
        to stop spinning!"

           "Who are you, gentle
      lady, who urges me
off Paolo?"

"I'm Marilyn
    of Tennessee.
      Chica, quick!

I've come to
    unplug you
      from this bad rap."

          "I can't leave
      Paolo!
  He needs me."

"Franny, get therapy!
    He was a one-night
      stand that seemed

eternal.
    Damn! What you did
      was stupid, no crime.

How many other women
    fell to Paolo's 'Let's read
      Lancelot' shtick?'

Love (or Handsome)
    seized you—*amor,*
        ch'a nullo amato amar perdona…

Being desired,
    that's what we women
        can't resist.

Your husband Gio
    could have subbed
        for the Mob.

His crime,
    your bones know.
        The bad-girl meter's up,

Sis,
    give it a rest.
        It wasn't God who pitched

you onto this whirligig
    with Dido
        and a flock of sexed-up birds.

It was a man, Dante,
    the exiled poet,
        whose wife Gemma dumped him

with two kids,
    no Florence,
        and a girlfriend

who channeled God.
    Honey, Hell's not
        always about you!"

The Dreaming World

At Red Cinder

"The only man in the house
        is Mr. Coffee!" the director jokes.
We women laugh with her.
        "That's okay."
At sixty, we agree.
Or pretend to.

Here on the island
        women's bodies hold sway.
                Pele appears barefoot at
the geologic station,
        disappears when
                helicopters try to rescue her
from eruptions.
        Reasonable men
                have seen her stir
in murals, have offered
        a white-haired woman a lift
                on the loop road. Her hair
brushes bodies
        in the tropical air, her dreaming
                wafts through screen doors.

Young boys
        fix their eyes on her.
Not that they want to
        sleep with their mothers, no—
they utter a language of respect,
        "Tūtū" "Nani,"
Dear, Beautiful.

Silver-haired dancers
   let down thick waves
      in the presence
of loved ones, enter the
   hula, calling with bodies,
      their hands echo
swaying
   palms,
      full hips in play.

Uncles with ukuleles
   croon to American women—
      someone is dreaming of us, too.
We are kin to undulant
   pines in the trades,
      to green, white, black sand,
to Pele, who one day

will take back not only night
but morning,
   the land that is hers,
      shacks and houses with good bones,
      the Red Cinder Road,
         on her way back to Nāmaka,
         Ocean Sister.

Pele is dreaming back,
   before men invented her jealous war
      with the sea,
dreaming of Women's Time—
   sisters draw stick families in sand
      and laugh like shore birds,
beckon dream-visions
   in the spirit of hula, weightless,
      fragrant as plumeria.

Even wild boars lie down
  drunkenly
    on banana leaves.
Here fire spells roasting
  and warmth. In the Dreaming World,
    before the descent beckoned.

Poli`ahu

If the snow goddess craved form   before name

   if she swirled herself into being   on Mauna Kea

If she cascaded into teenager

   nobody's cheerleader   tall even for god

   and cold   not like Pele

If she came roiling first

   then entered

   the whirlwind   of herself

Pele, older   stalked her

   like a bad boyfriend more than sibling

Who makes myths? At my house, me,

my sister,

       my Southern Mama   boiling over

       Montgomery beat down Brooklyn

in her drawl   orange hair   stiff cosmos

and red nails   summoning dogs and us girls

On Mauna Kea

Pele   surged through Poli`ahu   whose monster payback

came down   tsunami

    Sisters on the Island   fight   all time

    if you believe   *huhu*   (men)

Detached

Pele's sister Kapo possessed a detachable vagina,
unlike us. We can't distract
wild boars by flinging decoys. In high school, though,
I dated a guy with ADD, bristles, and pig eyes.

Unlike ours, Kapo's twat was detachable.
She could fling it like a Frisbee. Kamapua`a, the pig-eyed god,
never caught on. I dated a guy like that, dumb, bristles
on his back. One day he was buying me a charm bracelet,

the next, snorting, pig-eyed and dirty.
I'm not saying he was a gigantic eight-eyed hog like
Kamapua`a, but those black bristles down his back,
mood-swings and his rooting around my pants, marked him.

At South Side High, boys grunted like wild boars.
Lucky Kapo! Unlike us, she possessed a detachable vagina.

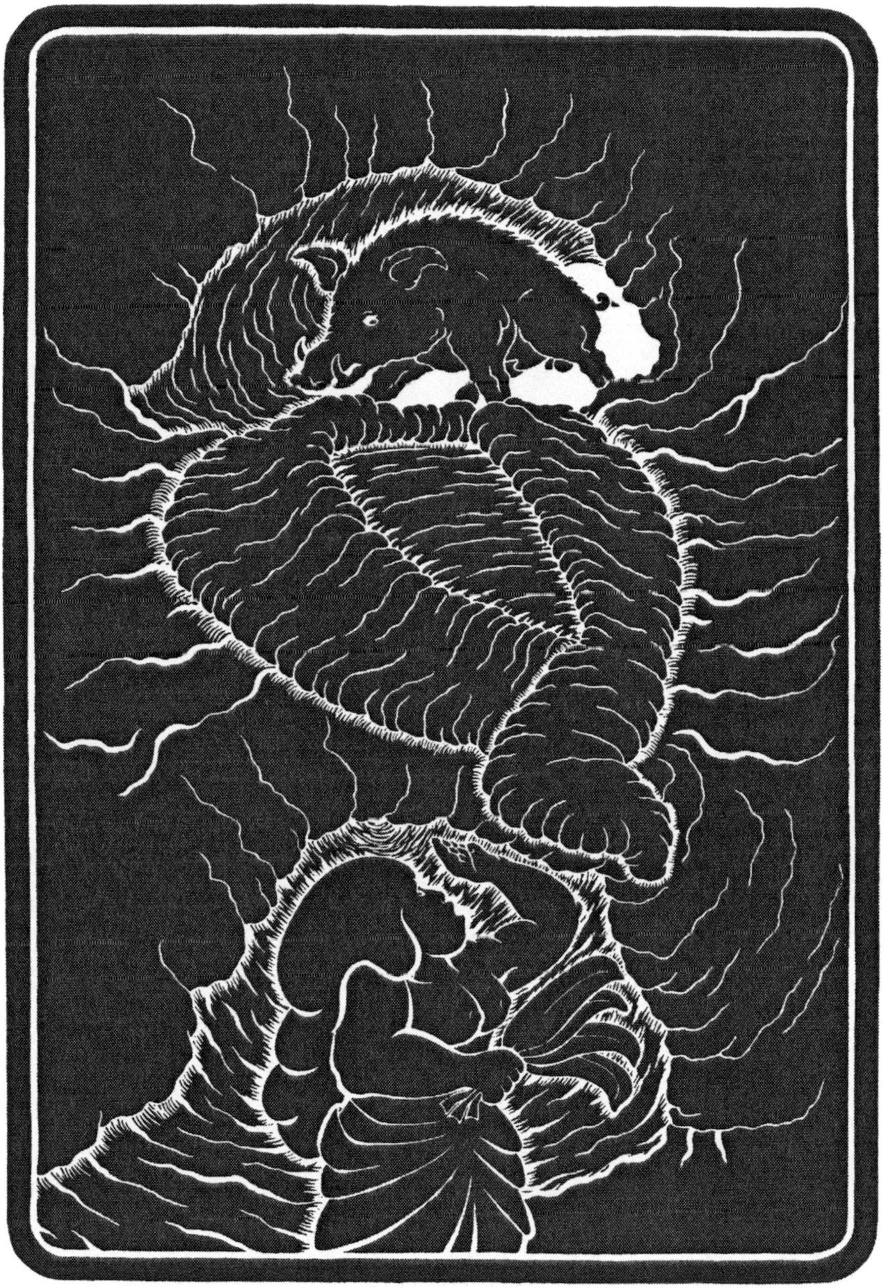

Kapolohelele © Dietrich Varez

No Dawn

There's no dawn
   no twilight
      on the Big Island
You wake up
   (you're lucky)
      sky's grey
blue
   bluer
      you eat sunny
papaya
   and apple
      bananas
You swim over
   green sands
      arm
over arm
   in the blue
      over black sands
with huge turtles
   more graceful than
you.

Keep your car locked
   alert
      for crackheads
young ones
   with dead
      eyes
they don't care
   Remember
      Mauna Loa's

schedule   pray
   it's not the same
       as yours
Remember
   "The island
       is a great teacher"
Search-and-Rescue
   does not rescue
       after dark
and "Hawai`i" can mean
   "Paradise"
       or "Land of the Dead"
depending on Pele,
   which way
       her lava flows.

Lines I Can't Cross

When I don't enter the lava tube,
I'm my father, stalled
at the mouth of the Lincoln Tunnel,
sweating and praying,

my Grandma Anna
locked in steerage, then in her airless apartment
on Coney Island, yellow paint peeling,
dreading Cossacks.

When I don't enter the lava tube,
I dream back, December 28, 1946.
They took me from my mother.
My bassinette, a hospital drawer.

There are lines I can't cross.
Kapu, Hawaiians say,
when the Marchers of the Dead
press in.

When I don't put on kneepads
and a helmet,
when I don't crawl back in,
when I don't enter the dark tube,

I'm Daddy. I'm Grandma.
God of spaces open and
narrow, God of desert
sun, sunless places,

help me be less narrow.
Help my daughter
live more fearlessly
than me. Keep her

resilient like the ohia,
first to grow back out of lava,
waving red blooms
over the shoulders of ghosts.

Witches

The poet wants to dream like Pele,
    but a flock of francolins
shrieks
    4:45 a.m.
The goddess had a purpose
    for them.
How else would coffee beans
    get harvested,
the pot brewed?
How would poets
    snap out of it,
stanzas
    be composed?

Francolins, you stir the
    roosters
who become our snooze alarms.
    You tickle the nenes,
wake
    grey light,
the women in the house,
    their arts—
why so loud?
Are you trying to rouse
    Mauna Loa?
You shriek
    like witches on crack.

You jumpstart
    us,
and *la,*
    our sun.

Sirens

The neighbor's baby goats wail like human infants,
bawl for milk, sound off
when they're afraid, when I run by.
They can't spot their mother.

Louder, they bawl for milk, sound off
as I jog by the wooly sirens.
When they can't see their mother,
these babies freak out. I'm their Godzilla.

As I jog by the wooly sirens,
my nipples tingle, hot
with milk-needles. I freak out—I'm 62.
Can't be! But this is summer, *Hawai`i nei!*

When they can't spot their mama, I'm Godzilla.
Neighbor goats wail like my long-ago baby girl.

Ode to the Malasada

Passion fruit icing slathered on top—"Have you tried the liliko`i?"
the young man behind the counter asked.
"That's why I'm back!" I grinned. "I'll write an ode
to these plump, tart doughnuts that bury Krispy Kremes."

The teen buttoned in Aloha bagged the liliko`i.
"Why chomp more than one doughnut for a poem?" he asked.
"Do I look like Proust? I write from life, not memory," I said.
"Even Marcel downed two or three madeleines for art."

"I need a second doughnut, a third,
to stoke my lines. You want Proust?
Oceanside, Long Island, was no Swann's Way, no
pastry pillows redeemed my youth."

"That's why I'm back!" I've brought my teeth & tongue
to the passion fruit icing slathered on top.

Ode to Ripe Papaya

Dressed in a gold jacket
on my black lacquered plate,

one easy slice—
your coral flesh

makes up
for no sunrise

wakes the tongue,
Komo mai,

welcomes back the body
like gentle *wahine*

and Aloha-spirited men,
"and that the truth

is in kindness,"
creaminess

in the little spoon that
prolongs you   helps me not gobble like a bear

or a New Yorker
No wonder these islands were fought over

if the Dole corporation won
we will lament   then

we'll ease more slices
down our gullets

with macadamia syrup
and coconut cream,

dream of mythic lovers we become,
crooning, "Taste this, Honey,

you won't need a spoon."

Blue Pie

Cobalt blue it landed,
loaded with aspic and whipped cream.
"Blue potatoes," the waiter
explained. We tucked in, sampled
the soft wall: potato mortar,
coconut bricks.

Picture the Aztec farmer
who pulled the first blue potato
like a musical note from the earth. His kids
mocked him—"Dad's a dreamer!
Who's going to swallow this?" His wife,
a weaver, fell in love
with the blue spud. "Potatoes
bore me," she said. "At
least this one offers
night sky, filling romance,
flavor for the eye."

"At least this one
makes me laugh
a little when I crave
more than mashed potato nights,
laugh a little
when I cry."

To the Roaches in the Rental Car

The moment my back turned you crawled into the pastries,
into the mango doughnuts, the passion fruit malasadas.
You're not babies, not new to this, you've been around
the rental car trunk a million times.

Into my pink mango donuts, into my passion fruit.
If you have crawled into my suitcase I will fry it.
Buy everything new.
You're obese, better fed than your New York

kin. If you have skittered into my carry-on you will
burn. I'll incinerate everything.
Fatter than your Lower East Side kin,
you dine too well on the Big Island.

Not babies, you've been around.
Moment my back turned you crawled into the creamy centers.

Taboo

"Pele, you snore!" I whine.
      "No one has ever
            complained!"
she growls.

      "Maybe it's because
            you're Pele-`ai-honua,
Pele Eater of Land,
      Pele Devourer,
            Pure Flame.
Remember Kalapura,
      1986? Uncle carried
            what was left
on a truck,
      and sighed, "I love my home,
            But if Tūtū Pele like
take it,
      it's her land."

Old Pele,
      searing
Queen
      of Unforgiving,
pipe down!

"Where you reside,
      risk level runs a mere six,"
            she snipes.
"Soon you may find
      yourself in
            waters by green
sands, and your
      number then will be

Zero. Molten.
You'll run uphill
   to escape Namaka's tsunami,
     into my
blazing arms!
   You won't have time
    to cry my other name,
Ka-`ula-o-ke-ahi,
   Woman of Flame,
    Fire's Heart.

Tūtū Pele
   never snores!
    I am Mauna Loa
and Kiluea.
   My fire's
    the last
     word in stone
your tender
   soles will touch,
    my heat will sear
your last
   rasping breath."

Uncle

"It never rains in Kaua`i," the resort manager bragged.
Then why am I soaked?
Blame fiery Pele's uncle,
Kamapua`a, for the morning storm.
He pushes his snout through lava-blackened soil.
Because of him papayas ripen.
If you're not guarded,
he'll slip into your life through a
dark-haired lover, he'll wreck everything.
Then he'll help the song-catcher
draw rainbows to your throat.

When I tell her about Uncle, Heather says,
"Mom, if I was child in Hilo,
would you put me to sleep with stories of a god
whose phallic snout causes chaos?"
"You loved Pinocchio," I point out.

Back home, Uncle K. strews mourners and babies
in his wake. Little mirrors of
his gorgeous mug. Though
he's been scarce for years,
his shit still fertilizes our garden.
From time to time some careless freshman
will mention his name.
Blouses come undone again, women
unbraid their hair.
Our garden prospers.
Worms love it most of all.
Me, I suck on it like a ripe papaya,
his name that is, rain in my heart, seeds
in my teeth, seeds in the dark rich earth
ready to explode, fire in the hold.

Woody Allen Mind

Kaua`i

4 a.m., alone, listening to robot
weather warnings:
"strong coastal wind advisory."

At the dock, a crewman grabs
our shoes. Tosses them on a pile.
Slippery ladder to the catamaran.

"Wait until the boat bumps back
to the dock and then—jump!"
Captain Andy welcomes us

aboard, yells, "Where's the Lot family?
They have the map. We can't go
anywhere without the map!"

Adds, "We have lifeboats
For…let's see…half of you!"
"Better odds than the Titanic,"

someone notes.
We sail against the wind
near the cliffs of Nā Pali.

"*Nā Pali*," our guide explains,
"means *Home of the Dead.*"
Of course, how

could it not?
Watch the Jewish girl cling
to the slick

deck
for dear
dear life.

Saffron Finches

So that's what they are, news
from the Caribbean.
If we call them wild canaries,
they don't care. They bob,
lively corks untroubled
by mad love or mortality.
They have their own
tsuras—hawks,
bulldozers chomping
trees, vacuums sucking up rushes.

Still they don't live like humans,
bickering and tormenting one another.
Osama means nothing to them.
With a whistle, they float
away from the thrum of
lawnmowers working the monster
hotels. Like poets they dream
of warbling,
strong currents of air.

Old Teacher

Japanese Meditation Garden, Hilo

The banyan rains down on Buddha,
trails of moss cascade
like the mane of a mystical horse.
Crows sound off like roosters,
waking the braid of garden and sky.
Long ago, French 101, Madame taught us
about *correspondances,* how heaven and earth

mirror each other, every material thing
a cup for the spiritual.
So much in love with her,
I copied out her *Saisons,* each poem
by hand. Became her best student,
until I left to study with another teacher.
Then she pronounced me dead.

Madame had opened the world for me
like a book of lyrics,
offered Baudelaire, music
of the cosmos, revealed
its poetical keyboard.
I'm told she's sick now.
What shall I say after thirty years?

"I have a daughter, too," I'll write.
"She's sixteen. How's your Eve?"
I won't add, "You
Didn't let her breathe."
I would only have to start again.
Isn't it hard enough to find
a few tender words for an old love?

Flamboyans

Honolulu

Brazen trees of Puerto Rico
and Wakiki, your
rouge blossoms
flaunt their beauty
like certain stylish women—Anaïs
Nin, Coco
Chanel. Shower trees
itch to get up and
merengue, intermingle
their stems and blooms.
Birds yearn to abide in you,
hang up their wings. Bees
lumber about, fuzzy
and fat like baby bears.
Me? I want to
be twenty-one again,
back in Acapulco, sunning
on the isle of shells,
with a rum punch
in my hand, and William Walkoff
leaning over me, long,
hard, and tan.

Pretender

The Big Island

Not every mountain can be
Mauna Loa, though this one's
pretty big. Its shrouded mouth
nurses on rainclouds.

You were no molehill.
Even close up, you looked good.
If doctors had measured my heart rate,
they would have guessed

I'd climbed high.
Never scaled you though.
No touching God.
Slippery mud.

Steep descent
without handrails.
Girls: let this teach you fear.
If he's too beautiful,

prettier than you,
steer clear.
I myself went mad.
Thirsty, weeping,

wild. For what?
Poetry?

Angel's Envy

Inferno Girl

"This silence is so thick not even God can bite it," Francesca pouts.
"I'm already in Hell (Canto V). What else can go wrong?"

One night on the adultery Tilt-a-Whirl she glimpsed
Paolo gone. How long had he been AWOL?

She called out to him, scratched poems, her pages fanned
ash on the Inferno Grill dance floor.

Pecked at blank wall, cooed, sighed.
Nada. One denizen advised,

"Once you give up, success begins." The damned
were always spouting things like that.

But she stopped bitching. Did Paolo care?
He'd taken up with a closer pigeon.

Who could be closer than the one
he'd been boning for eternity?

The new girl in the poetry workshop,
at the Café Shock and Betray.

Paolo's story is smoke, Cuban cigars and mirrors.
He'll come back when he needs cash, Francesca swears.

The moment she renounced hope she grew
dazzling to other men, Romeos

once fierce like Paolo, now Chia Pets,
grizzly, overgrown. No day spas at Inferno.

Francesca warbles continual surrender. Old men
latch onto her like blackbirds on a scarecrow.

Not until she's emptied herself of his name
will Paolo return with lattes and burnt offerings.

His name is her nemesis, her Attila,
her Malfoy, her silky, adorable shade.

D & B, Bickering

A blip on the road to Paradise   Dante & Beatrice are bickering
something about clamshells on the dining table   he says it's
   French
she says disgusting

she's not polite
about the limp salad
I'm not impressed, she sulks

she's not the one paying
a little less heavenly she'd be boring
little less River of Heaven in her hair

intolerable
less drop-dead
gorgeous she'd be

gorgeous
you can't look at her and not think God
that was the plan, mates

make your peace with beauty
Dante's taken
so are you

don't leave your carcasses on the table
you can't stop beauty
or even slow it down

you want to bury Beatrice
you can't   there are always more
men who buy in

become Dante?
so not easy
still   the road to heaven   beckons

hell looks good too
Euro-Disney
buy your ticket   before the lady's Big Top folds.

Treachery

Beatrice never caught Dante with a blonde.
No need, Dearie.
Sky Cat kept his boys in line.

If Dante drew near
someone unbeatific,
Whiskers bared a steep maw.

One day Dante veered toward alien strands.
Curtains! cursed the stars.
Bea tripped over her crystal ball.

She didn't wish him well in his new new life.
La vita nuova was good enough for her,
why wasn't it his gelato?

She stuffed herself, burrowed in.
How had she failed him?
By wrinkling a mortal body?

Grandcat couldn't hear complaints, grasped
only traps and cheese.
She wasn't mousy.

Spat at the fresh fluff,
"Beat it, Sugar, or I'll crunch
your skinny bird bones,

bat you round like baby NASCAR!"
Bea was mean empty.
Dante seemed gaunt without her.

She'd spoon him pomegranate pie
until he spilled syrup,
lick his sticky tips, & her paws.

Dante, Back Door

If not highway, I
was his
rural route to God.

He was a backdoor man,
in mind,
you understand,

he wrote and wrote until
I was sore.
Sorely tried.

I need someone
younger,
he said.

I'm nine, I said.
I don't have women friends,
he swore.

It's God, ecstasy,
or I is someone
with someone else,

out the door.

Speed Demon

The city morphs faster
than the human heart,
unless it's Springfield, Illinois,
where the Olive Garden still
sustains the action.
The poet's racing heart is his
and hers. And hers.
But that's Orpheus.
He's not mercenary,
doesn't make a dime.
Makes time.

Soaked

At the friary lunch we chat about End of Days,
and who was at the Last Supper. John and Peter

to the left of Jesus, Judas clutching his moneybag,
verklempt on the right, Mary Magdalene. I'm playing her—

splashy red-rose dress and Jewish sarcasm.
Bro Jesus at our table is Latin, too good-looking.

When he confesses he has a poem to share,
I'll be damned if I swoon. I pitch San Juan's "Poem

for the Ascent of Mount Carmel," stained
with the poet's erotic sweat for God.

Old Father Conrad flashes snapshots of his macaw,
that he has trained to shriek, "Praise the Lord!"

He ministers at the cancer ward—no one begrudges him
a flamboyant bird in his room.

No one but Benjamin Péret, and he's crammed
between acid-free pages of a paperback.

Sometimes in the morning my desk is wet
from condensation of the water glass.

But I dream Benny's been here, spitting
from the grave at every priest he spies,

soaking them like a loaded Surrealist
in the day. Now he drives the bus to Père Lachaise.

What happened to you, Benny,
in that vestry in la Vendée, behind those heavy

curtained robes?

The State Trooper Behind You is Not a Surrealist

He's Tennessee's Finest, his blue blinking lights
relentless. Too slowly you suspect he's trailing you.

Now he's Surrealist in bulk, in beige khakis.
His mug looms twice the size of yours, framed

in your Hyundai window.
You were speeding, of course, on the way

to meet your poet sister for the retreat. So?
Flirting with him won't help, he's no Paul Eluard,

no Picasso. He's Dada but not Dadaist, alas,
and he sticks you with a yellow sheet of misery,

not because you're a Yellow Dog Dem
and he no doubt voted early for Santorum,

no, the trooper issues a "moving and non moving" citation
that could cost you your license and your first-born.

You won't know that until three days later,
when you pop open your glove compartment and

study the arcane page that indicts you.
Not the Da Vinci Code, Tennessee circuit court law.

But for now, I-75 unfolds more Romantic than
Surrealist, redbuds all pinkish fuzz on skeletal twigs

mislead you into creating automatic writing with your car.
I-75 is not driven by someone else, you're the one lulled

by lush green, and though you're transporting a bottle of
Angel's Envy—unopened—only the angels grasp

what's moving and unmoving at once. Your sapphire car
amuses them. Trooper Larry clocked you

going fast, but to the angels you're merely
a slowpoke, though they are never unmoved by your plight.

They cannot intercede with Officer Larry, this is no Heaven
Hill, no Mayberry, so you will have to ponder the one

and the many, moving and non, on your own,
revisit that stony face violating your driver's side,

in flashbacks at your desk, with branchwater
over ice, in a stretch of long lines that frame Officer

Dada's massive ass in your adjustable rear-view mirror.

Eurydice in Nelson County

Eurydice streaked the black Del Sol
through backwoods snow.

She'd trekked through hell before
but this fell whiter and colder than

Jersey. The Lovington Food Lion
roared with freaked-out country folks,

hoarding bread and pad Thai.
What to do? Go slow, pray?

"There ain't been no God of Israel in these parts
since Job was a boy," Cuz said.

The grey man at the end of the driveway leered,
"I told you so." According to the Nelson County

Mortality Schedule, he'd been dead long enough to know.
Eurydice planned to track poems and down Bordeaux

until the sun came back, or
Orpheus phoned. After all this time,

would she know his voice if the call
went through? She'd made mistakes before.

Soon as the sky cleared, she would find him,
above or below.

Orpheus Down Low

Orpheus craved a three-way, freaked Eurydice.
No matter the other slice was Hedy Lamarr,
voluptuous beyond body. She came on wavy and salty.

Eury was narrow. She could follow
one thread without a GPS, but not a sloppy goddess.
She'd been dissed.

No, she cried, but the bad boy stayed busy,
other line.
He glowed almost human, rosier

than nips in Hades.
They had braved brimstone, Orph and Eury.
He showed no loyalty.

Wrapped in whispers. Unless
Eury layered the club sandwich,
she'd be dumped outside the cave, days

before May took hold, when a cold shoulder
could still slaughter
babbling springs and buds.

Sorcery

Just the word *wood*
made Eurydice swoon.
But it wasn't words
that drew her, or the lyre. She
was stuck on his rock-climber's body. He could
bolt her out of this pit, flash up the narrow
chute. She'd wrap her legs around him
and he'd forget his shaky
Elvis knee, the ages she'd been
wasted. She knew how to fold a man
in the cocoon of her hair
and silk him down.

He never called. Stone stoppered the cave
mouth, and Ali Baba signed with Disney.
She tried to whistle but her lips
cracked. The tunnel kaboomed
in 1970.

The only orifice was dream, so she aimed
her ribbon of song. The tabby
on the master bed turned an ear to the ripple.
Orpheus leaned in, so rapt
he thought he was Rilke, on leave
from Countess Marie. Then reverie
secreted something about black silk,
black cherry lipstick,
the hardwood cherry sideboard
in his dining room.
Gleaming, it lured him.

Puritan

Maybe he hated adoring her
Maybe his passion spooked him
Maybe he had to tie himself down
Maybe her name ignited him

Maybe his obsession cornered him
Knocked the air out of him
Maybe her name freaked him
Maybe she died like ash on his lips

Knocked the breath out of him
Maybe she was alive, lithe
He turned stone and ash
His lips cruel like an ancient statue

Maybe he had to topple himself
Maybe he adored hating her, his teacher.

Cons

Don't con a conwoman, Eurydice lipped.
    The gig she hired Orpheus for was cushy,

touch of sweat, some nights.
    Liar and lyre, she thought.

Eury was into bad boys long after her
    Retired Underground Groupie pin arrived.

She was paying the big O a stud fee,
    though there was no *shtupping* involved.

Just crooning. He could belt a lyric.
    If eagles boomed like Pavarotti,

that would be him. His footing sure
    as any mountaineer. And his hair

made Eurydice want to tumble backward
    into hell, never mind the eons

it had cost her hand-over-hand to climb out.
    She wanted to scale him

but that could happen only
    in measured sighs.

What could she offer her boy
    besides overtime?

Eternity is in love with the
    productions of time, and Honey

he was an extravaganza.
   Encore! She plunged again, again,

like her saggy skin.
   If she had trapped him in her

descent-into-personal-hell
   work-study program

he was agile enough to
   ascend, leaving her

rock bottom,
   her bottom no rock,

sagging in her capris,
   in the downturned

economy, her only skill
   an ancient come-hither look

that used to make cocks cry
   & point like weathervanes.

The Charm

Days when we snatched occult books from Hempstead Public
        Library, Caren and I
needed voodoo. We were poor and poorer, my father ranted,
        Ma swallowed it.
C's parents were divorced. My mother forbade me to see her.
        We met on the sly,

on the roof of her apartment, or in the woods off Merrick
        Road, where the "bum" lived.
We had hit twelve, made out with Italian boys, Sal Noto,
        Angelo Gatuso.
What we wanted—thought we did—were older hoods with
        cars. Lucky for us,

they despised Jews. Banned us from their souped-up Cameros.
Mango Sherbet lipstick triggered our mothers' cries, "Like
        tramps!"
"Don't leave the house like that!" We punched up our pout with
        white gloss.

Didn't get us far. So we stole a striped sweater from a preppy
        store, freaked out—
what if one of us got caught wearing the booty in Mrs.
        Heugler's homeroom?
Ditched it in a curbside can. We needed magic, something
        potent, something sure.

The Encyclopedia of the Occult. At the library, power arrived
        alphabetized—Alchemy to
Zulu Witch-finders. Nabbed it in my bag. Under A: Amulet
        of Venus. The spell
called for copper, a magician-and-engraver, the face of the
        legendary Planetary Genius

Suroth, favorable signs. I rang the Hayden Planetarium about
    Saturn's aspects.
"Is this an astrological question?" the operator groaned. We'd take
    our chances
with the stars. Called the Village co-op, "Anything for Anybody,"

where dreamers like me and Caren could spell out desires. Left my
    home number,
our list of ritual needs. "We're driving to Coney Island to see
    Grandma,"
my father said. "Can't," I said, "I have work to do. Tonight's a full
    moon."

Chomping at Nathan's, though, I fell under the spell of dogs and
    buns.
My father hiked to a phone booth to check messages. "Fourteen
    magician-
engravers called!" he said, puzzled. I babbled the story.

"You're not my child!" Mother spat out, as we headed home on Belt
    Parkway.
1960, Ma was the lion, the witch, and the discount wardrobe.
Years later, when a poet offered me a love charm, I took it. She had
    knitted a green

pouch to cover red seeds. All I had to do, she said, was wear this
    close to my heart,
dip the amulet in the beloved's drink. But I could never figure how
    to dunk a tit
in someone's coffee without being scalded. Luckily I met Lou,
    charmed already.

And Caren? She stopped caring—after her first husband joined
    Primal Screamers
on Staten Island, and her second, the lawyer, morphed into the Pig.

120

Complaint

Surrounded by
my designer
products, how
can I die?

Decleor for my
face, Coach
for my credit
cards, I'm headed

for Eternity.
Though yesterday
when the pimply teen
at the Johnson City

Wendy's offered
me the senior
citizen's discount,
I was crushed

for a sec.
Today in
fleet Nikes
& Adidas racing pants

I'm back,
outstripping
my own best time.
Only my

downcast
boobs
toll an elegiac
note.

Dog Days

Gigi, my mother's miniature,
barked at Volkswagens.
"And she hated the smell
of coloreds!" Mother bragged.
No black people

came to our door
on Coleridge Road. None
permeated the perimeter.
Mom had planted a black jockey
on our front lawn.

One block away, whites only
caddied at the Club.
We Jews weren't allowed
in the swim.
You would have had to be dead

not to smell the fear
that soaked my working-class childhood
like a sprinkler in the fifties,
our soggy upper-middle crust
in the sixties,

and after. Was it fear
that turned our collie
mean? Mama had Lady
"put to sleep."
And if she was kinder

to the cute poodle than to the rest
of us, who could blame her?
When I was four, Mama
permed me
to look like her toy.

My scalp scalded, hair fried.
Scared straight since.
Dogs were better at obeying
than we were, better
at unconditional love.

Lady aimed to kill everything
that moved.
Spared Mother's hands, though.
Licked her Alpo-scented fingers,
bathed and bathed those tough red nails.

Easy Listening Music, I-75

My father liked "easy listening
music"—everything else had been hard,
Work was his birthright.
His mother Anna scrubbed floors,
carrying her youngest. Harry.
His older brothers had opted out—
a small-time crook, a big shot
with Murder Incorporated. No wonder
my father was neat—no grime,
he was proud of his fingernails,
clean little moons over clean hands.

Why do I gather clutter?
Here she is, my Grandma Anna,
standing in the narrow aisle
of her second-hand store.
Anna, saver of old sweaters, mothballs,
pogroms hidden under mounds of cloth.
She hid her guitar on top of the hall closet.
We kids would have been embarrassed
to hear her sing Yiddish,
eager as my mother was to rise
to middle-class brightness.

What songs did my grandmother
take with her from Russia?
At fifteen, did she sing her mother's
lullabies in the ship's hold?
Croon them again to little Harry,
to Nat, and Sammy, and my frightened
                            Aunt Marilyn?
Were there other babies who didn't survive
hungry nights in Coney Island?

Markers for Indian mounds slip by,
this ground I ride easily over.

The Jewish graves are dispersed,
of Anna I have
no traces—only me.
I want to be a song my grandmother
would have recognized.

Rest a little, Harry.
Sleep, my little Anna,
Shayn viday-la vo-na,
pretty as the moon.

Running with Elitist Dogs

My squeaky Reeboks defy the lords
   around Harrison Keepe, circle

too subtle for a gate, the name aimed
   at peasants like me.

I'm musing teeth and titles I can't use—
   "Night of Desirable Objects,"

some rock band nailed that,
   "Lure," landed by a hack in Kansas City.

Starter castles are girdled with manicured lawns.
   Their hounds wag, friendly as mutts

from Long Island childhood.   But our bitch,
   Lady, bit little Raymond Lafosse, whose daddy

used to punch him.   My jaw's sore.
   I'm grinding molars.

Biters thrived in our clan.   Uncle N, hit man
   for Murder Inc. in Brooklyn, sprinted

into a new name and a trailer in California.
   Three strikes.   No way he'd revisit Sing Sing.

His wife Ina, 300 pounds, shoplifted her mini-Frigidaire.
   Their boy Sonny cooked a smack O.D. in junior high.

Cher, the Good One, taught special children.
   Who'd blame her for name-changing to Ariana,

reading runes in the Haight, doing good
    at Harvey Milk Civil Rights Preschool.

My emails bounce back. Last link to my father's
    family, she refuses to be tagged.

Chivas and Hannah, golden gals, grow calm
    when they spot me. I crumble the Milkbone

under Hannah's purebred nose.
    The retrievers bow.

Though I know it's an evolutionary ploy,
    they've had more schooling

than many of my kin—Grandpa picked spuds
    in Minsk, Grandma Anna was too busy fleeing

Cossacks to wring history from books—
    I don't hold it against pups, easy to read.

Chère Ariana, runner par excellence,
    envision me tracking, calling you,

reinvented one on the run from blood
    and memory.

My voice a streaming ribbon
    against San Francisco blue, summons you

through runes you're deciphering
    bit by bit, like our bloodline, like our poem.

Dr. Robert Darwin Weighs In

The boy's a drifter—I pulled him from Rev. Butler's
for low grades, being excessively lazy. "Son," I warned,
"you care for nothing but shooting, dogs, and rat-catching,
and you will be a disgrace to yourself and your family."
His classmates called him "Gas Darwin," after his
chemical experiments in our shed. Shipped him to medical college,
Edinburgh, no small cost. Two years, bored. He learned taxidermy
from a South American blackamoor, prattled about exploring
the rain forest. Stuttered like an odd bird, "Wha-wha-wha-wha,"
I turned him toward the clergy and Christ's College.
His latest scheme? Sail round Cape Horn to pick bones.
"Charles," I advised, "another career change looks suspect.
You'll sleep poorly in a hammock above the stove. Don't go!"

Confined

Emma expects to be confined in March,
a period I most devoutly wish over.
—Charles Darwin, Letter to Fox,
January 25, 1841

Honestly, Charles has worn me out.
I won't be sorry to find my bed.
He can whine more than fat little William.
With his misery of headaches and chills,
how did he survive Rio Negro
and Cape Horn? His father was dead set.
The sea looks shiftless on a resume.
Charles claims our house is ugly, brags
about fifteen acres, quinces, plums, Spanish chestnut
and old larch, nine miles from Knole Park.
Cook says I'm carrying a girl. We'll name her Anne.
Neighbors drop carcasses—dogs and cats—
in our foyer, and Charles cheers them on.
I dreamed Annie was a ruby, burning to the touch.

My Dear Emma

> April 23, 1851
> *Nature is cruel, man is sick of blood.*

"I quite thank you," Annie said, when I offered water.
The fever appearing very bad does not kill one.
In Malvern, six or seven *severe* cases, not one died.
Dear Emma, how to prepare you?

Fever should not have killed our spirited child.
When does a parasite hook on? Why this sweet girl?
She thanked me.
What fragile blood did I bequeath? Her breath

fell, tranquil. Our sweet girl was never mean,
never whined, "Where's Momma?"
"Please don't," she said reasonably, when I tried to move her.
In January, Annie suffered "two fretful cries."

Then she grew "well" awhile. I read aloud Lamartine's
Genèvieve, and a *Boy's Country Book,*
both pastoral. Two fretful cries do not imply
inherent evil. Our household joy, gone.

How to swallow a severe species of God?
I offered water. "I quite thank you," Annie said.

Before   (September 10)

The night before the end of innocence
the lights of Houston Street glimmered.

The firemen had not yet mingled with the ashes.
Now there's Before and After,

stairwells, smoke,
relatives clutching photos,

buckets, hand over hand,
the smell of flesh.

Those on the highest floors had not yet
streamed into their ending,

unfinished, falling like love letters
they had barely begun.

The night before the air was shattered,
the watchmen had not begun to speak of war

or revenge.

Yom Kippur Remembrance

They were not love letters, they were
people, someone's mother, another's son.
Brave enough to leap, cheat fire,
some of them hand in hand.
This Yom Kippur we pray for
their families, for those "hurt,"
the rabbi says. Pray for the "wounded,"
she repeats. *Mi shebareach l'avosaynu.*
Bless those in need of healing.
Does our language mock them? Do we need
new words for images burned into our brains—
no, "burned" is a lie.

Yisgadal, v'yiskadash. Praise God.
We are the living. What

will be the legacy of our heroes, who raced
up stairs to help others and crumbled
under fiery rubble, under some fanatics'
idea of fame? Yom Kippur, we let go
of anger, quiet it the way we'd calm a sick child.
We forgive, ourselves, the vague ominous world.
Forgive God. Free will, the rabbi says.
The ashes fall again, forgive men's hands.
We see God in the faces of the
rescuers, she says. I believe her.

Don't write about disaster, our Poet Laureate says.
We know what happened. Tend the ordinary.
I believe him, pull dead leaves
from the mums. Miracle-Gro for them.
Sunlight and fasting for us.

Eating the New Species

Port Desire. Ship's artist Conrad Martens shot the prize. Baby ostrich, Darwin thought. "Merry Christmas!" He downed the bird with bread and tinned peas. Savoring the last morsels, Darwin's memory returned. "Save the bones!" he cried.

"Their minds are so like ours," he noted, of the natives, among them his friend Jemmy Button. "What's for dinner?" Jemmy teased. Along with his instruments, Darwin packed a bible, a pistol, and a "peacemaker" club for disputes, like some who would later deny him in Tennessee.

1833, Darwin ate his homework. Later he watched his children on the playground and studied the expressive macaques. 1920, the jungle gym was invented in Chicago, to satisfy "monkey instincts." Darwin walked a "thinking path" every day at Down House.

No coffins prime time. We can watch the interrogation of weeping sixteen-year old Omar at Guantanamo. "You don't care about me!" he moans. So what? He wasn't waterboarded. "Learned helplessness," invented by a psychologist, is an important tool in the war on terror. As to torture, "History will not treat us kindly," John Ashcroft swore. December, Port Desire, Darwin wrote, "Certainly, no fact in the long history of the world is so startling as the wide and repeated exterminations of its inhabitants."

Spleen

I am eating dirt today, gravel-filled bricks of dirt.
Hard to swallow, even if pre-chewed.

Someone's squatting over me. No,
it's the gritty shadow of my blunder looming

like a TV soap opera. And I'll need that soap.
So I'd better keep my mouth open—too late

to keep it closed.

Today the Underworld

Today the underworld rises to the ordinary,
dons earth and sky lightly as if everything's okay—
Fourth of July sparklers, bombshells.

No one's dead, right? Dad's ashes so long gone
they don't whisper.
Mom, well, Mom.

Stink bugs in the towels of Virginia.
Locks popping,
middle of the night.

That well-known poet who made promises,
is jammed up, prepping for eternity.
Do not read Plath on such a day,

or drive by your old friend's house at Sweet Briar.
If she wouldn't talk to you before the slaughter
in the rented dining room

why bother now?
The ordinary says go call the plumber.
Write your name on your half-empty wine.

The great poet who once adored your work
models "no." Her afterbite
champs like heavy machinery on mute,

like the pretty world
pretending
not to be ripped in two.

Climbing Solo

At the bend where the James meets the Tye,
I summoned you to skyline above
two rivers. Better that we're impossible
like this, spaces between us wider than geography.

I thought of you, your legs lifted me
the last four miles. You won't know this.
Better we're impossible, not even close,
miles above the swirl where rivers embrace.

You'll never know that your legs
lifted me over tangled miles of scrub, cold wind
swirled my hair, briars bit my jacket.
You would have made it to the summit.

Better that we're impossible, miles above
the tryst of the James and the Tye.

Almost

I almost made it to the promontory,
stopped short, like Moses,
and me without wisdom or flock.
Terrified to look over.

I stopped. Unlike Moses I had no mission,
no rod, just my snakelike thoughts.
Afraid to look over.
Cossacks coming, rapists, Nazis, God help me,

I heard all my mother's warnings. No snake,
just my own fears to stall me.
God help me, no Pharaoh, no Dark Lord,
just me in the pretty wilderness,

backcountry Tennessee. Without wisdom or flock,
I almost made it to the top.

July Notebook

hi eternity are you still in love
with my productions?
how's ben péret?
fuck eternity he says
words only

the retired racehorses
ben and fella are easier
than some
writers   clear
about what they want
apples   carrots

the poets want fame
the straight male poets
want fame
and young women
the young women
want what they want

poetry
is no place for whining
ben says   tell your words
to put their cards
on the table
and on the desk
and the forest paths

the bobwhites
agree
or whatever they are
robert hass would know
he's not here
eternity is love with him
and so are

the cards
shut up and deal
ben says
he's dead so I
listen to him
an egg dances out
of the kitchen

God Particle

(2007)

1. Particle/sanctuary
   (Mount Saint Francis)

   First day
   　　　　a flock of goldfinches

   bop
   　　　　from the bushes

   like buttered popcorn,

   　　but soundless.

2. "What does it do?"

   "Acts like cosmic molasses."
   If I say not tonight,　　　　(fall apart without)
   I feel like I have particles
   in my *kopf,*

   you'll know I mean mystical blackstrap goo—
   the missing stuff, yo-yo, you.

3. The Higgs or 'God particle'

    is named after Peter Higgs.
    His wife wanted no part.
    He'd say "Honey, come 'ere, I've got a big bang
    to show you," and she'd lip,
    "Take your tiny shifting short-lived
    particle and shove it!"

4. Dark Matter

    Scientists call it dark because they can't see it.
                        You went dark in 2004.
    How do you find it then?

    You don't.
    But scientists are prepared.
    They should be able to notice its absence.
    Anyone would.
                        Cell
                        not throbbing—

    Every particle has a heavier sibling.
    No one has ever observed these hefty partners,
    though.

    Big fatties.
                        Godfather particles.

5. Mini-black holes

High-schoolers on the beach, 1950,
Far Rockaway. Hair-pulling fights
with Joanne Scraffidi
over Angelo and Johnny.

Scientists agree they're a long shot.

They wouldn't live long.

They're extra tiny dimensions to space-time maybe,
matchbook dollhouses, your parents still alive,
blue hydrangeas, sprinklers, the house
on Vincent Street standing.
You light the little rooms with fireflies
and call yourself in to bed. You won't need supper.

Like Moonlight

> "Without the Higgs field…matter
> would zoom around at the speed of
> light, flowing through our hands like
> moonlight." —Dennis Overbye,
> *The New York Times*

absence streams
through our hands like moonlight

not finding you
God-damn particle

then you sent the poem
the God particle

we planted iris bulbs
and watered them

all night rain of music
or at least a couple of hours

yes, we timed ourselves
human

we'd flow through each other
heaven

without words how would we
stop?

Angel's Envy

For Barbara

The last poem wrapped antique lace around an oak tree.
Didn't care about rain and time, nonchalance one key to its

charm. The last poem held first love and last, lover and husband,
the same. The last poem netted the creature clawing

in the attic and set it free. The last poem flew down by
the lake and joined its mates, veered north for the summer,

and the lake's response created mist that none of the women
had glimpsed before, not a ghost-mist, more moon-infused air.

The new moon was not jealous of the last poem.
The wren on Saint Francis's head did not trouble the last poem.

If it left a white mess in the saint's hair, the rain took care of that.
The last poem offered air, cool and fresh, perfect for late March.

The last poem held two women saying goodbye, one parting for Mass,
then home to Muncie, the other preparing to brave a night alone

in the old House of Prayer. Tomorrow the last poet will wend her way
back to Tennessee, and pray not to attract another speeding ticket,

she will offer thanks on her way out the door—thanks to the friars,
to the lake and the beings trapped and free,

thanks to thickets of bird song and wildflowers, to the ticks
who didn't attach themselves. The last poem is a shot of Angel's Envy

and a clear glass of water, not a chalice,
a sip of praise.

NOTES

The Love That Moves Me varies Dante's *"amor mi mosse, che mi fa parlare."* ("The love that moved me makes me speak.") *Inferno,* II, 72. Virgil repeats to the Pilgrim, Dante, lines that Beatrice has spoken about the source of her actions and speech.

For a graceful English translation of Dante's journey to the underworld, see Robert & Jean Hollander's *The Inferno,* Anchor Books, 2002. My citations from *The Inferno* are from this edition.

Preface

"Baudelaire was my boyfriend..." Charles Baudelaire (1821–1867) was a French Symbolist poet who lived in Paris, one of the first modern poets. Jeanne Duval, "Black Venus," and Marie Daubrun, the actress, were two of the women Baudelaire loved and mythologized. Apollonie Sabatier, the courtesan, was the third female muse.

Section I.

"Exclusive" opens the refrain from a song, "Je M'en Vais," by Christophe Miossec.

"What Would Baudelaire Do?" The last three stanzas revisit Baudelaire's "Enivrez-vous," from *Le Spleen de Paris,* 1869. My poem also refers to another Baudelaire prose poem, "Any Where Out of the World. N'importe où hors du monde," *Baudelaire: Oeuvres complètes,* Gallimard, 2012; 1975; 337; 356-57.

"The Revolution" opens with a refrain from a Beatles' song found on *The White Album.*

"You Are What You Haunt" plays on the French adage, *"Dis-moi qui tu hantes, je te dirais qui tu es"* ("Tell me who you haunt, I will tell you who you are.") André Breton explores the theme of "haunting" or mutual obsession in *Nadja,* 1928.

"Playing André" refers to Surrealist André Breton and his younger friend, writer Joyce Mansour. Mansour inspired Breton, and they traveled together, but remained platonic. In his later years, Breton wanted to protect his marriage, according to Mark Polizzoti's biography, *Revolution of the Mind: The Life of André Breton,* Black Widow Press.

"When" opens with a translation of the first line of another "Spleen" by Baudelaire: *"Quand le ciel bas et lourd pèse comme un couvercle..."* *Les Fleurs du Mal,* LXXVIII, 1861, Gallimard, 74.

"Storm Warning" reframes Baudelaire's line from "Spleen": *Je suis comme le roi d'un pays pluvieux."* ("I am the king of a rainy country.") *Les Fleurs du Mal,* LXXVIII, 1861, Gallimard, 74.

"Pitiless" ends with *"greee,"* a sound repeated by Michael McClure in "Ghost Tantra #1 (1964)".

"Sad History at Dunes"—this narrative was given to me by Moïses Baratto, in 2007, when I first stayed in Auvillar. Moïses died in 2009, and is survived by his wife, Odette.

"I Am the Wound and the Knife," translates *Je suis la plaie et le couteau,"* from Baudelaire's "L'Héatontimorouménos," *Les Fleurs du Mal,* LXXXIII, Gallimard, 79.

"Tous les êtres aimés…" ("All the loved ones / Are vases of bitterness that one drinks with eyes shut.") The lines are from Baudelaire, *Poèsies diverses,* "A Sainte-Beuve," Gallimard, 208.

"In the Shade of the Nuclear" opens with *"stries,"* or "streaks," the opening word of Chantal Bizzini's poem, "Carte Postale."

"In the Shade" includes a statement by Hitoshi Sato, quoted by Martin Fackler in *The New York Times,* "Japan's Quake-Prone Atomic Plant Prompts Wider Worry." 2007/07/24.

"Leaving the House"—the epigraph is from Adrienne Rich's poem, "Prospective Immigrants Please Note," from *Snapshots of a Daughter-in-Law,* 1963.

"Few Talk" offers details that are also available on the website *Mémoires et Espoirs de la Resistance.* The site includes narratives by Jewish Resistance fighters. Much of the information in my poem comes from the testimony of Dr. Jean Raphaël Hirsch, who served in the Resistance when he was nine. A retired physician, he lives in Paris, and is still bearing witness.

"The Love That Moves Me"—see opening note.

"Freeing Francesca" takes for its epigraph a line from J.P. Miller's song, composed for Kitty Wells, in 1952. The song was banned on NBC radio, and at the Grand Ole Opry.

"Freeing" includes Dante's opening words from *Inferno,* I, *"Nel mezzo,"* as well as Francesca's line, *Amor, ch'a nullo amato amar perdona.* ("Love, that pardons no beloved one for loving…") *Inferno,* V, 103.

Section II.

"At Red Cinder" includes "Tūtū," an affectionate term for a grandparent.

"Poli`ahu" uses the Hawaiian word, *huhu,* which means "angry."

"Detached" revisits a line from *Pele: Goddess of Hawai`i's Volcanoes,* by Herb Kawainui Kane: "Kapo…happened to possess a detachable vagina."

"Lines I Can't Cross" mentions ohia (`ōhi`a), hardy native flora of Hawai`i, the first to come back after volcanic eruptions or tsunamis.

Kapu means forbidden.

"Witches" speaks of francolins, large, beautiful, insanely noisy birds, about the size of pheasants. Nenes (nēnēs) are Hawaiian geese; the nene is the state bird of Hawai`i. The last stanza includes *"la,"* the Hawaiian word for sun.

"Sirens"—*Hawai`i nei* means "Dear Hawai`i."

"Ode to the Malasada"—These are Portuguese doughnuts, popular on the island. Liliko`i are passion fruit-flavored, to die for. My favorites are found at Punalu`u Bake Shop.

"Ode to Ripe Papaya"—*Wahine* are women. *E komo mai* means "Come on in!"

"Taboo" mentions the "threat level." Property in "lava zones" on the Big Island are assessed on a risk scale from one through nine.

The quotation from "uncle" comes from Kane's *Pele: Goddess of Hawai`i's Volcanoes,* 7.

"Old Teacher" mentions *"correspondances,"* or connections, referring to the ideas in a poem by Baudelaire, in which every material thing has spiritual and poetic resonance. Baudelaire was influenced by Swedenborg's ideas.

Section III.

"Speed Demon" begins with a line loosely translated from Baudelaire: *"la forme d'une ville / Change plus vite, hélas! que le coeur d'un mortel."* ("The form of a city / changes faster, alas, than the mortal heart.)" *Tableaux Parisiens,* LXXXIX, "Le Cygne," Gallimard, 85.

"Soaked"—Mount St. Francis is a Franciscan friary in Southern Indiana, where I often go to write.

Benjamin Péret (1899–1959) was an unrepentant Surrealist who used to spit on priests in Paris. I translated his *Le grand jeu (The Big Game),* and he had a habit of visiting my dreams. I apologize to my friends, the Franciscans!

"Cons" holds a quote from William Blake's "Proverbs of Hell" *(The Marriage of Heaven and Hell),* "Eternity is in love..."

"Dr. Robert Darwin Weighs In." *The Autobiography of Charles Darwin.* W.W. Norton, 1958, 28.

"Confined" (1958). Darwin *Correspondence Project,* Letter 586, Darwin, C.R. to Fox, W.D. [25 Jan 1841] http://www.darwinproject.ac.uk/entry-586.

"My Dear Emma," holds an epigraph from a translated line in Lamartine's *Geneviève*. Annie's lines were quoted in *Darwin, His Daughter, and Human Evolution,* by R. Keynes, 2002, 89–90; 217.

"Eating the New Species," refers to Darwin's account of eating a petise, a rare bird, by accident. *Zoology* 2, Part III, 1839. Reprinted in *Charles Darwin's Beagle Diary,* Cambridge University Press, 1988, 212.

"Certainly..." *The Voyage of the H.M.S Beagle (1838–1843),* New York: The Heritage Press, 1957 Edition, 158.

"Like Moonlight," was inspired by Overbye's article on the successful discovery of the Higgs Bosun particle at Cern, published in *The New York Times,* 7/5/12, A6.

"all night rain of music" is from Denise Levertov's poem, "A Tree Telling of Orpheus," found in *Relearning the Alphabet,* New Directions, 1970.

"Angel's Envy"—In bourbon-making, the whiskey that usually evaporates from the barrel has been called "the Angel's Share." Recently, Lincoln Henderson in Kentucky has produced a smooth bourbon from this distillate, and he calls it Angel's Envy.

Marilyn Kallet
is the author of sixteen books, including *Packing Light: New and Selected Poems,* Black Widow Press, 2009. Her translations of *The Big Game,*

© Christophe Gardner

by Benjamin Péret, 2011, and *Last Love Poems of Paul Eluard,* 2006, were also published by Black Widow Press. Kallet is the Nancy Moore Goslee Professor of English at the University of Tennessee, where she directs the Creative Writing Program. She also teaches poetry for the Virginia Center for the Creative Arts in Auvillar, France.

Kallet has been awarded the Tennessee Arts Commission Literary Fellowship in Poetry, and she was inducted into the East Tennessee Literary Hall of Fame in Poetry, 2005. She has performed her poetry internationally, as well as in theaters and on campuses across the United States.

TITLES FROM BLACK WIDOW PRESS

TRANSLATION SERIES

A Life of Poems, Poems of a Life
by Anna de Noailles. Translated by Norman
R. Shapiro. Introduction by Catherine Perry.

Approximate Man and Other Writings
by Tristan Tzara. Translated and edited by
Mary Ann Caws.

Art Poétique by Guillevic.
Translated by Maureen Smith.

The Big Game by Benjamin Péret. Translated
with an introduction by Marilyn Kallet.

Capital of Pain by Paul Eluard.
Translated by Mary Ann Caws, Patricia
Terry, and Nancy Kline.

Chanson Dada: Selected Poems
by Tristan Tzara. Translated with an
introduction and essay by Lee Harwood.

*Essential Poems and Writings of Joyce Mansour:
A Bilingual Anthology*
Translated with an introduction by
Serge Gavronsky.

Essential Poems and Prose of Jules Laforgue
Translated and edited by Patricia Terry.

*Essential Poems and Writings of Robert Desnos:
A Bilingual Anthology*
Edited with an introduction and essay by
Mary Ann Caws.

EyeSeas (Les Ziaux) by Raymond Queneau.
Translated with an introduction by Daniela
Hurezanu and Stephen Kessler.

Furor and Mystery & Other Writings
by René Char. Edited and translated by
Mary Ann Caws and Nancy Kline.

The Inventor of Love & Other Writings
by Gherasim Luca. Translated by Julian and
Laura Semilian. Introduction by Andrei
Codrescu. Essay by Petre Răileanu.

La Fontaine's Bawdy by Jean de La Fontaine.
Translated with an introduction by Norman
R. Shapiro.

Last Love Poems of Paul Eluard
Translated with an introduction by
Marilyn Kallet.

Love, Poetry (L'amour la poésie)
by Paul Eluard. Translated with an essay by
Stuart Kendall.

Poems of André Breton: A Bilingual Anthology
Translated with essays by Jean-Pierre Cauvin
and Mary Ann Caws.

Poems of A.O. Barnabooth by Valéry Larbaud.
Translated by Ron Padgett and Bill Zavatsky.

Poems of Consummation
by Vicente Aleixandre. Translated by
Stephen Kessler

Préversities: A Jacques Prévert Sampler
Translated and edited by Norman R. Shapiro.

The Sea and Other Poems by Guillevic.
Translated by Patricia Terry. Introduction by
Monique Chefdor.

To Speak, to Tell You? Poems by Sabine Sicaud.
Translated by Norman R. Shapiro. Intro-
duction and notes by Odile Ayral-Clause.

forthcoming translations

*Boris Vian Invents Boris Vian:
A Boris Vian Reader*
Edited and translated by Julia Older.

Pierre Reverdy: Poems Early to Late
Translated by Mary Ann Caws and
Patricia Terry.

Jules Supervielle: Selected Poems
Translated by Nancy Kline and Patricia Terry.

MODERN POETRY SERIES

ABC of Translation by Willis Barnstone

An Alchemist with One Eye on Fire
by Clayton Eshleman

Anticline by Clayton Eshleman

Archaic Design by Clayton Eshleman

Backscatter: New and Selected Poems
by John Olson

The Caveat Onus by Dave Brinks

City Without People: The Katrina Poems
by Niyi Osundare

Concealments and Caprichos
by Jerome Rothenberg

Crusader-Woman by Ruxandra Cesereanu.
Translated by Adam J. Sorkin. Introduction
by Andrei Codrescu.

Curdled Skulls: Poems of Bernard Bador
Translated by the author with
Clayton Eshleman.

Endure: Poems by Bei Dao
Translated by Clayton Eshleman and
Lucas Klein.

Exile is My Trade: A Habib Tengour Reader
Translated by Pierre Joris.

Fire Exit by Robert Kelly

Forgiven Submarine by Ruxandra Cesereanu
and Andrei Codrescu

from stone this running by Heller Levinson

The Grindstone of Rapport:
A Clayton Eshleman Reader

Larynx Galaxy by John Olson

The Love That Moves Me by Marilyn Kallet

Memory Wing by Bill Lavender

Packing Light: New and Selected Poems
by Marilyn Kallet

*The Present Tense of the World: Poems 2000–
2009* by Amina Saïd. Translated with an
introduction by Marilyn Hacker.

The Price of Experience by Clayton Eshleman

The Secret Brain: Selected Poems 1995–2012
by Dave Brinks

Signal from Draco: New and Selected Poems
by Mebane Robertson

forthcoming modern poetry titles

An American Unconscious
by Mebane Robertson

Eye of Witness: A Jerome Rothenberg Reader
Edited with commentaries by Heriberto
Yepez & Jerome Rothenberg

Memory by Bernadette Mayer

LITERARY THEORY /
BIOGRAPHY SERIES

*Revolution of the Mind: The Life of André
Breton* by Mark Polizzotti. Revised and
augmented.

LOUISIANA HERITAGE SERIES

New Orleans Poems in Creole and French by
Jules Choppin. Translated by Norman R.
Shapiro. (*Forthcoming* from the Second Line
Press imprint)

WWW.BLACKWIDOWPRESS.COM